Usborne
Sticker Dolly Dressing
Travel

Illustrated by Steven Wood
Written by Fiona Watt
Designed by Non Taylor

Contents

Meet the dolls

Meet Tilly, Lola and Erin, three dolls who love to travel and are always planning a trip away. Where will they decide to travel to next?

Tilly enjoys being outside, whether she's wandering around a city or doing something sporty.

Lola loves taking photographs of the places they visit and carries a camera with her everywhere she goes.

Erin likes to read guidebooks so that she knows something about the place she is visiting.

At the airport

The dolls are getting their boarding passes at the automatic check-in machines at the airport. They will still need to drop off their luggage and go through security, before boarding their plane.

Ferry crossing

The dolls are standing on the deck of a ferry that is taking them to a sun-drenched island. Lola has her camera ready to take pictures of the village houses as they sail into the port.

Hiking trip

The dolls are tired after a day hiking along forest trails. They're now relaxing at a lake-side campsite, chatting about all the fantastic things that they've seen and done today.

Vaporetto in Venice

The dolls have arrived in Venice, an Italian city on an island, where there are no roads or cars. The only way they can explore is to walk through the narrow alleys or take a water bus or *vaporetto,* that zigzags between stops along the Grand Canal.

Snowmobile

Tilly's had a freezing but exhilarating ride on the back of a snowmobile. She had to hold on very tight as it sped across bumpy ice and powdery snow.

Riding adventure

Erin adores horses and is spending a week riding.
Every day her trek leader takes the riders along
winding trails, through fields, across shallow
streams and down gentle hillsides.

Seaplane

The dolls have had an amazing trip in a seaplane. As they soared above the islands, they had incredible views of coral reefs and white sandy beaches. They even saw dolphins jumping and diving in the crystal clear sea.

Intercity train

Tilly, Lola and Erin are on their way home after a week having fun on the snow at a ski resort. They took a bus down from the resort high in the mountains and are continuing their journey by train.

San Francisco cable car

After a long day sightseeing, the dolls are tired so have decided to wait for a cable car. Erin has read in her guidebook that it's a good way to travel around the hilly streets of San Francisco.

Bus trip

The dolls are waiting at a bus station for the overnight bus that will take them on a long trip. Their large bags will be stored in the luggage compartment beneath the bus.

Cycling tour

Erin, Lola and Tilly have joined a cycling tour where they ride to a new place everyday. The tour manager takes the girls' bags onto the place they will stay each night so they don't need to carry much and can enjoy the cycling.

Travel journal

Some photos we took in a photo booth during our trip to San Francisco.

SAN FRANCISCO CABLE CARS

FULL FARE RECEIPT

1 RIDE ONLY

A snowman we made while taking a break from snowboarding in the mountains.

20

Lift pass

Valid for 5 days

9781409549703

Trying to look cool on the beach after our amazing trip in a seaplane.

Suiker
Zucker
Zucchero
Azúcar
Sugar
Sucre

Ferry crossing

Hiking trip

Vaporetto in Venice

Pages 10-11

Snowmobile

Riding adventure

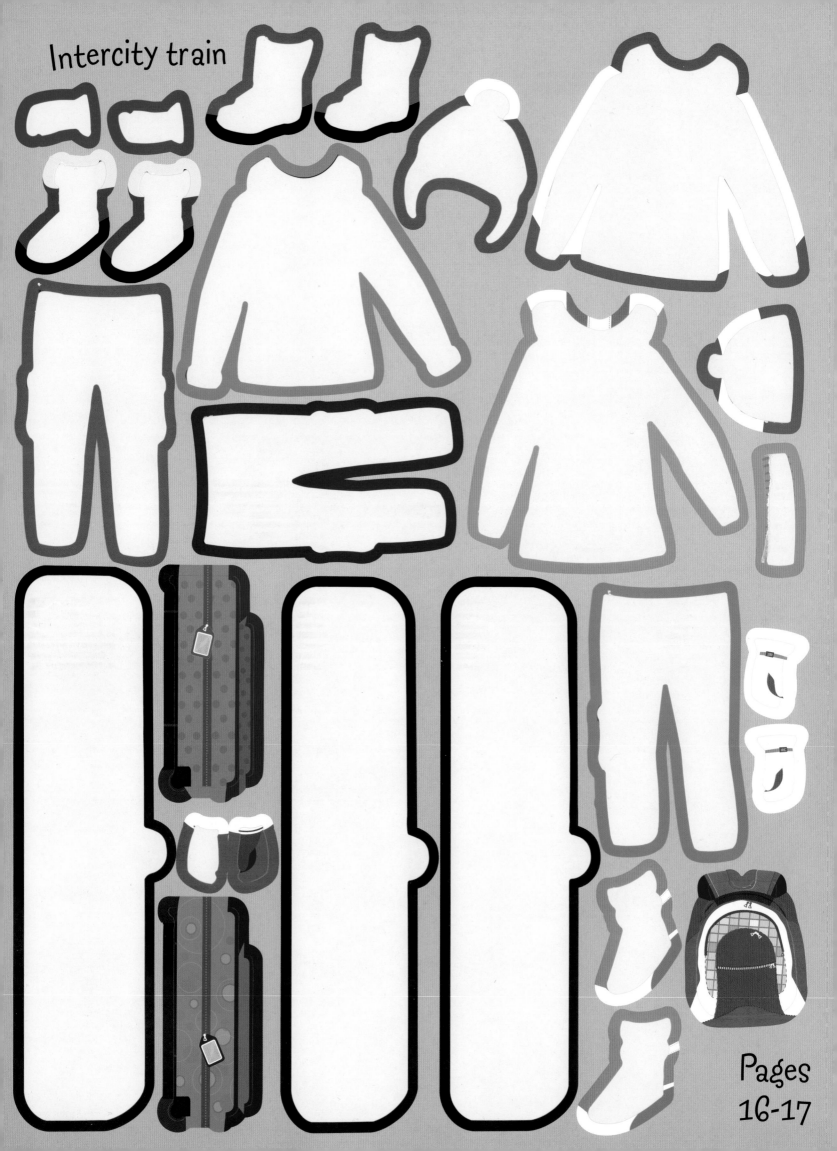

Intercity train

Pages 16-17

San Francisco cable car

Bus trip

10B

Cycling tour

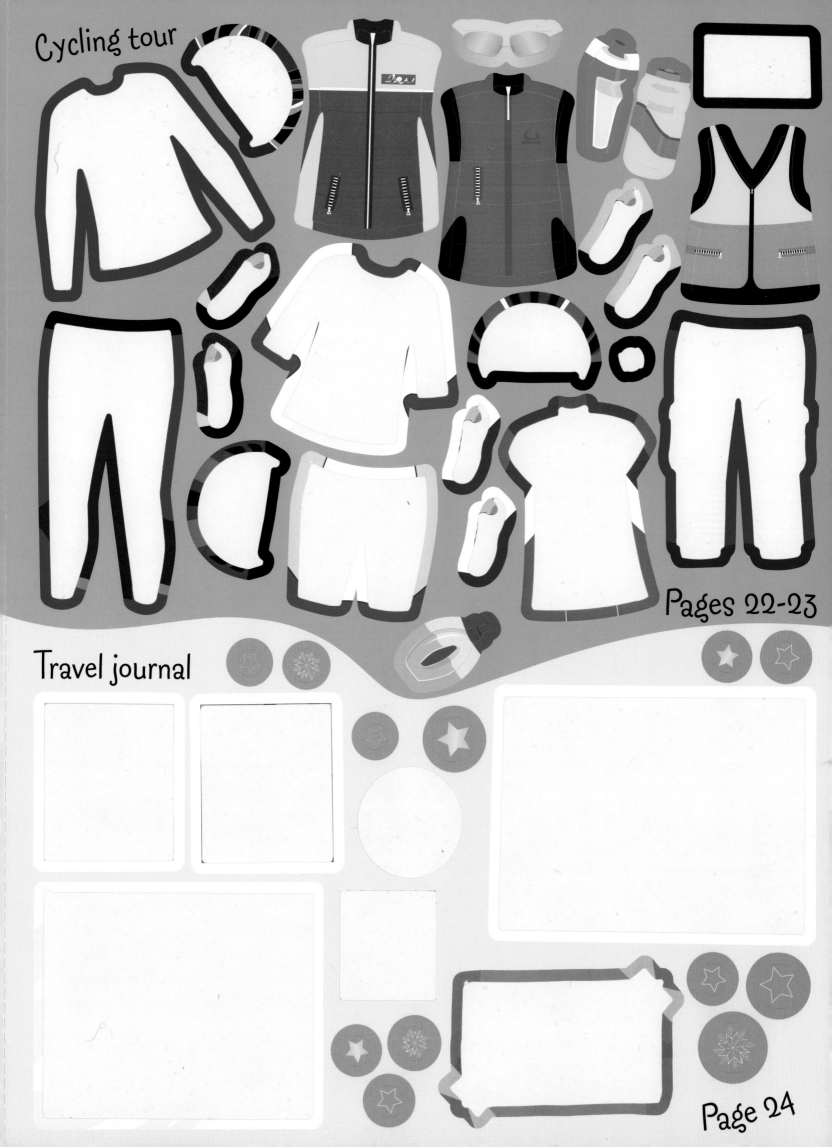

Pages 22-23

Travel journal

Page 24